painted
furniture

painted furniture

Making ordinary furniture extraordinary
with paint, pattern, and color

Katrin Cargill

photography by David Montgomery

painting by Tabby Riley

A Bulfinch Press Book
Little, Brown and Company
Boston New York London

For my brother Jumbi, and Juliet and
the girls, with love

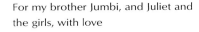

Text copyright © 1999 by Katrin Cargill
Photography and compilation copyright © 1999 by
Ryland Peters & Small Limited
Kimono flowers page 119 copyright © 1999 by Museum of
Fine Arts, Boston, Massachusetts

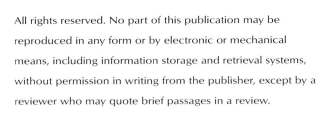

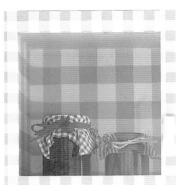

First North American edition
First published in 1999 in the United Kingdom under the title
Contemporary Painted Furniture by Ryland Peters & Small
Limited, London, England. All rights reserved.

Library of Congress Catalog Card Number 98-75319

ISBN 0-8212-2541-3

Bulfinch Press is an imprint and trademark of Little, Brown
and Company (Inc.)

PRINTED AND BOUND IN CHINA

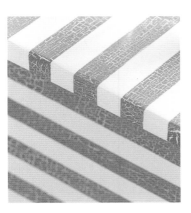

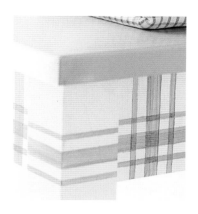

contents

from the beginning

For centuries painters around the world have left their mark on furniture, from elaborately gilded pastoral scenes on mirrors to plain numerals on school chairs. There is nothing new about painted furniture—indeed, there are many books on how to recreate traditional paint effects—but with the emergence of more pared-down interiors today, coupled with a growing selection of flat-packed and unfinished furniture now available, I feel there is a need for a simpler approach to this craft. For this book I have drawn on techniques and ideas from the past; patterns from everyday items, even natural surroundings, have influenced several projects. Painting furniture is fun, and you don't need to be an artist to try it. Be inspired by colors, patterns, and objects that you really love—don't be afraid to experiment.

Color schemes can be determined with the aid of old textiles: this collection of red, white, and stone-gray Irish linen influenced my choice of colors and decoration for the kitchen (*see pages 46-60*).

This antique patchwork quilt is highly decorated, but on closer inspection its pattern is quite simple. The geometric star in the center was the inspiration behind the sunburst bathroom shelf on page 90.

gathering ideas

Flea markets and thrift stores make great hunting ground for ideas. The mix of light blue, indigo, and white on these tin cups provided the inspiration for the crested garland box on page 78.

Flowers are probably the most commonly used motifs on painted furniture. Petals have a geometric perfection that suits stenciling and stamping in a repeating fashion.

Polka dots have such a jolly appeal. They fall into that rare category of simple but chic, earthy yet elegant. This blue pot from the Haute-Savoie in France gave me the idea of painting gold dots on a candle sconce (*see page 22*).

Botanical themes offer a huge source of inspiration. The pattern of falling leaves on this cool-colored ceramic soap dish evokes feelings of light summer evenings.

The colors and patterns in this section are inspired by the palette of Scandinavia: pale aqua blues, grays, and greens. The patterns are easy to achieve, and the techniques vary from printing with a sponge roller to rustic wood graining. All the ideas can be adapted to different sizes and styles of furniture by scaling up or down.

eating and

entertaining

dining table
folk flowers

This simple repeating stylized motif takes its inspiration from the painted exteriors of rural Norwegian farmsteads. The cheerful naïve painting on window frames, shutters, and doors, usually in just one or two colors, lends itself well to furniture. Here, a pine country table is painted soft cool lichen green, with a panel of paler green in the center. An egg-yolk yellow flower motif is printed with a cutout sponge and then outlined in darker green to accentuate the pattern. The flowers are printed around the sides of the table as well. The central decorated panel still looks pretty even when the table is set. Color is all-important here; the brightness and depth of the yellow paint is what give this very simple pattern its strength. A paler yellow would get lost in the greens. If you decide to use colors that will suit your color scheme, remember that the flower motif should be strong and bright, and the table colors more receding and muted.

materials

Wooden dining table

Lichen green and pale green water-based eggshell paint

Egg-yolk yellow and dark green concentrated artist's acrylic

Household paint brush

Soft-lead pencil

Metal ruler

Masking tape, low tack

White conté pastel stick, sharpened to a point

Black permanent marker pen

Sponge roller refill

Craft knife

Flat oil-based varnish, extra pale

Varnishing brush

preparation

Table should be sanded, acrylic primer undercoat applied, and painted with 2 coats of green water-based eggshell paint

1 Mark center panel

Using a pencil and ruler, mark a panel in the center of the table, making sure the distance in from the edges is equal all the way around.

2 Mask off center panel

Put strips of masking tape all around the outside of the pencil line for the central panel. Smooth down the tape with your fingers to prevent the paint from seeping under the tape.

3 Paint center panel

Paint the panel pale green by filling in the masked-off area, going over the masking tape slightly. Use long brush strokes to blend the paint. Let it dry. Paint again, remove the tape, and let it dry.

4 Divide panel into sections

Using a conté pastel stick and ruler, draw a 1¼-inch-wide band inside the panel (the same diameter as the sponge roller refill). Divide the band into evenly spaced sections.

5 Cut out flower stamp

Using a black pen, draw the outline of a flower on the end of a sponge roller refill and cut it out using a craft knife. Dip the end into yellow paint and dab off any excess. Print flowers in alternate sections around the panel. Let it dry..

6 Highlight flowers

Using a fine-tipped artist's brush and dark green paint, fill in the center of each flower and add tapering swirls around the edges of each flower.

7 Paint a green border

Using a pencil and ruler, draw equal lines on each side of the panel edge to create a narrow strip all the way around. Put strips of masking tape along both pencil lines. Using a square-ended brush, paint between the two strips of masking tape with the same dark green used to highlight the flowers.

8 Print side panels

Draw a rectangle (the same diameter as the
sponge roller refill) on each of the drop
panels around the table. Divide the
rectangle into sections to fit the flowers.
Print and highlight flowers along each drop
panel in the same way as before. Let it dry.
Rub out the white pastel marks. Apply
2 coats of varnish to finish.

swedish flowers

materials

Wooden chairs

Blue water-based eggshell paint

Pale blue and ivory concentrated artist's acrylic

Household paint brush

Tracing paper

Soft-lead pencil

Masking tape, low tack

Fine-tipped artist's brush

Clear flat-finish acrylic varnish

Varnishing brush

preparation

Chairs should be sanded, acrylic primer undercoat applied, and painted with 2 coats of blue water-based eggshell paint

Scandinavia is the European home for rural painted furniture. So many wonderful pieces exist in the many living museums that it is hard not to be inspired by their charming ideas. These pretty Swedish-style chairs need little embellishment, and for this reason I have kept the pattern very simple: just a two-color motif across the back slats. The beauty is in the strong cool blue base color of the chair coupled with the lighter blues of the pattern. There are many inexpensive unpainted chairs available, often rather crude-looking in unfinished wood. The transformation by paint is so satisfying, you'll soon be infected by enthusiasm. If you have a motley assortment of dining chairs collected over the years, in different colors, woods, or shapes, you can paint them all and transform them into a handsome set. For fun, the pattern is echoed in the seat cushions as well. The garland pattern has been slightly adapted to fit the cushion and painted with colorfast fabric paint on a subtle checked blue cotton fabric.

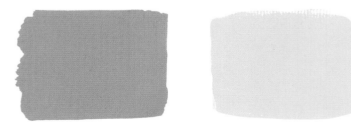

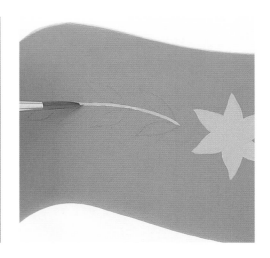

1 Transfer motif to chair back

Trace the motif (see page 120) onto tracing paper. Tape the tracing paper to the crossbar of the chair so the pencil lines face down and transfer the image by drawing over the design with a pencil. Remove the paper and retrace any faint lines.

2 Paint petals

Using pale blue paint, color in the petals with a fine-tipped brush. Remember to paint slightly over the pencil outline to cover it up.

3 Paint stems

Following the pencil guidelines, paint fine stems running between the flowers using pale blue paint. Remember to paint over the pencil lines to cover them up.

5 Add ivory dot to center of flowers

For the top seat back, enlarge the flower motif on a photocopier so the flower will sit comfortably on the chair back. Trace the motif, apply it to the chair back, and paint as before. Dot ivory paint in the center of each flower. Apply 2 coats of varnish to finish.

4 Add leaves to stems

Paint the leaves using pale blue paint, making sure you go over the pencil lines. Let it dry.

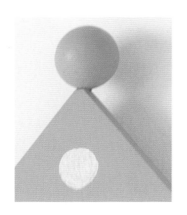

candle sconce
gold leaf dots

materials

Wooden candle sconce

Gray-green water-based satinwood paint

Household paint brush

White conté pastel stick, sharpened to a point

Metal ruler

Button, coin, or washer with ¾-inch diameter

Hard-tipped artist's brush

gold-leaf paint

preparation

Sconce should be sanded, acrylic primer undercoat applied, and painted with 2 coats of gray-green water-based satinwood paint

Gilding has formed the backbone of paint-decorated furniture for centuries. Think of the countless gilded mirrors, picture frames, and ornate furniture—lovely in the appropriate setting, but in a pared-down interior, all that gold can be too much. Swedish interiors seem to make gold work. Their secret is in using very little of it, and mixing it with lots of plain flat color. One of the prettiest effects often seen in Swedish dining rooms is their use of candlelight reflected in mirrors or gilded wall brackets. This modern wooden candle sconce emulates this effect with the use of gold-leaf paint. When the candles are lit, the light dances and reflects off the golden dots. The secret with gold leaf and silver leaf is in its subtlety—a little goes a long way; just the odd glimmer of gold can look magical in evening light. To determine the size of the gold dots, try different-sized coins or washers, by outlining in white conté pastel and seeing if the size suits the scale of the sconce.

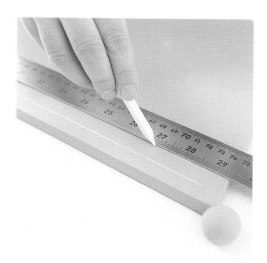

1 Draw parallel lines

Mark conté pastel dots along each side of the sconce about ½ inch in from the edge. Join the dots to create a line all around the edge of the sconce. Repeat for the second line, this time 1½ inches in from the edge.

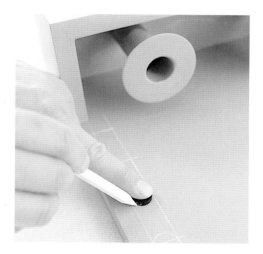

2 Draw around button

Mark a dot at the bottom of each side of the sconce, about ¾ inch up from the base, then mark dots 1¾ inches apart. Draw a horizontal line through each dot, put a button or coin over each line, and draw around it.

3 Paint gold circles

Fill in the circles with gold-leaf paint using a hard-tipped artist's brush. Let them dry. Remove the white pastel lines.

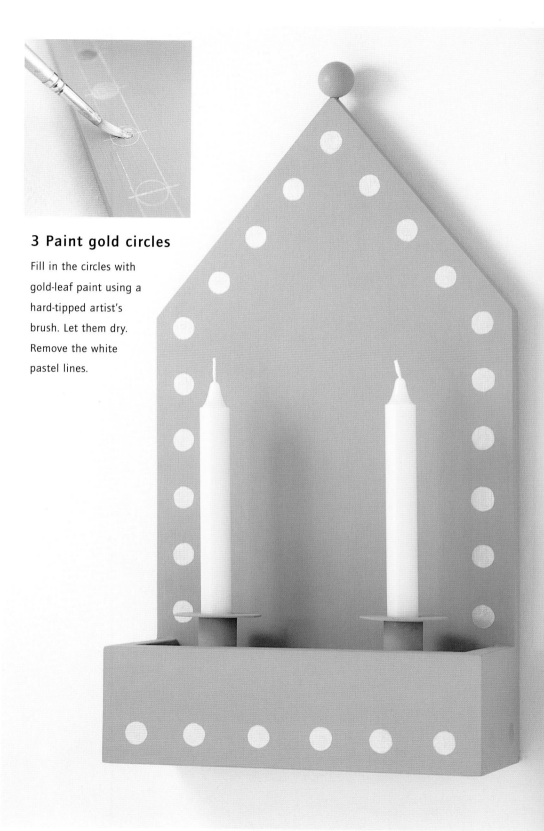

hanging shelf
rustic graining

materials

Composite board shelf

Cream oil-based eggshell paint

Household paint brush

Decorator's tape

Oil-based scumble glaze

Olive green artist's oil paint

Stippling brush or dusting brush

Lint-free cotton cloth

Rubber-ended brush with wedged tip

Flat-finish oil-based varnish, extra pale

Varnishing brush

preparation

Shelf should be sanded, acrylic primer undercoat applied, and painted with 2 coats of cream oil-based eggshell paint

A quirky paint effect for a quirky hanging shelf! Wood graining has been around for a long time, usually seen on soft and cheaper wood to make it look more expensive or unusual. Good wood graining cannot be distinguished from the real thing. Often painters in the past did not know what woods looked like, so they invented their own interpretation, and many examples can be seen on rural painted furniture such as trunks and chests. But to me the charm of a more naïve and fanciful graining is very attractive. The pattern created is crude, rough, and wonderful—the lovely thing about this graining technique is that you don't need years of training, and you can create your own pattern as you go along. However, because you have to stipple and grain over wet paint, you need a certain amount of speed and dexterity, so practice first on scrap wood or cardboard. It is important to work on one section of the shelf at a time and let it to dry thoroughly before you move on to the next part. Drying time will be long when using an oil-based medium.

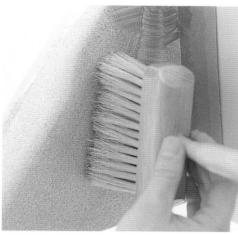

1 Apply tinted scumble glaze

Tint the scumble glaze to a desired depth of color with the olive green paint. Using a household brush, paint the tinted scumble onto a masked-off section of shelf.

2 Stipple painted surface

While the tinted scumble is still wet, use a stippling brush to stipple the painted surface. It is easier to control the stippling if you hold the brush upright and grasp it at the base of the handle. Remove the tape.

3 Wipe edges clean of paint

Using a damp, lint-free cotton cloth, wipe off any excess scumble that may have gone over the edge of the painted area—this will give the edge a neat, clean base on which to apply the tinted scumble later.

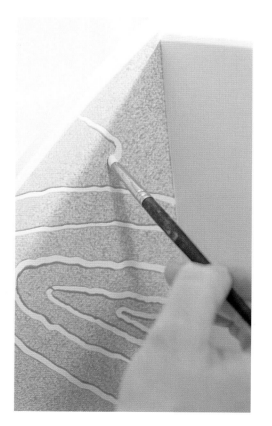

4 Imitate wood grain

Using a rubber-ended brush with a wedged tip, add swirling patterns in the wet scumble to loosely imitate wood grain. Hold the brush lightly so you can achieve slightly uneven lines. Wipe the excess scumble off the brush with a cloth as you go along. Remember to bring the lines over the edge of the shelf to continue the wood grain effect. Let this section of the shelf dry. Repeat the masking, painting, stippling, and line-drawing process for the inside of the other vertical strut.

5 Continue wood theme

Mask off the top shelf and paint, stipple, and draw in lines as before. Change the angle of the line as you turn the edge to match the vertical struts. Repeat for the other shelves and the outside of the struts. Let it dry. Apply 2 coats of varnish to finish.

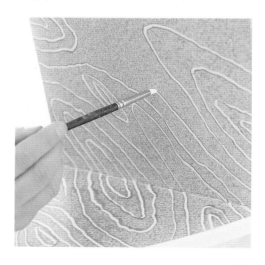

enhance with cool colors and

Accessories painted the same color unify items in a room, like these pale gray candlesticks and a wooden tray.

A pine country serving table has been given a wash of watered-down paint: gray-blue for the top and white for the base. Diluted colors will give a large piece of furniture a light and contemporary feel, especially when used in a pale color scheme.

pale washes

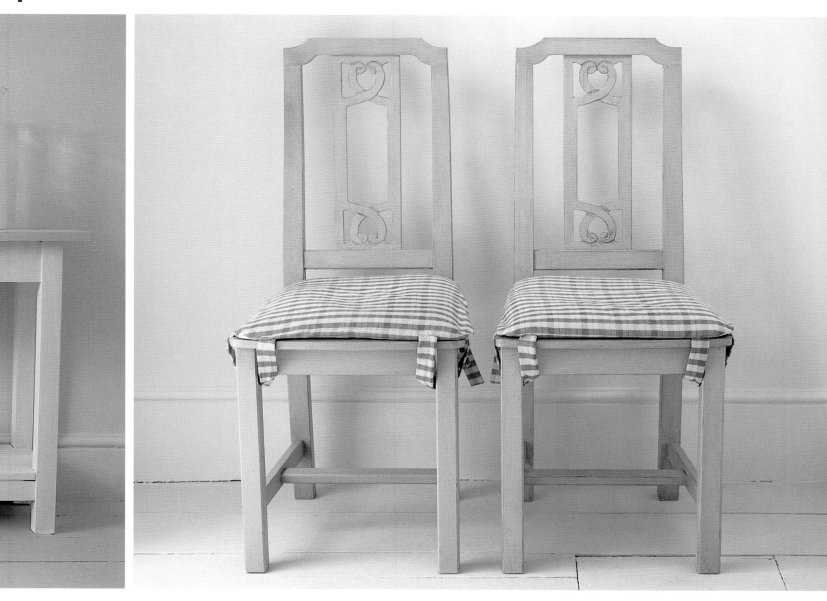

A pair of classical Swedish dining chairs painted traditional Scandinavian gray are complemented by the red country check of the seat cushions. This shade of gray is cool and sophisticated, which enhances the elegant shape of the chairs. Using a subtle, unobtrusive color such as gray in the background allows stronger colors to stand happily in front.

This section contains a diverse selection of old painting tricks interpreted in a modern way. Traditional methods, such as mosaic and comb painting, are used on modern, simple pieces of furniture to create a cool, contemporary look in the living room.

unwind

and relax

wooden sofa
combed squares

Combing, a traditional American decorating technique, was used by folk artists in the 18th century to create patterns by dragging a combing tool through a glaze. The principle remains the same today, but a modern look can be created by exaggerating the process to dramatic effect with wavy lines, zigzags, checks, or swirling patterns. Here, the geometric pattern of wavy lines has turned a plain wooden sofa into a striking piece of furniture. Color combinations are endless; using a dark-tinted glaze over a pale background will look more attractive than a light color on top of a dark one. Using a water-based scumble glaze reduces the lengthy drying time associated with an oil-based glaze. The clever use of an ordinary window cleaner's squeegee to make a combing tool means that you don't need to spend a lot of money on specialized equipment. It also means you can cut out the comb's "teeth" to the width of your choice.

materials

Wooden sofa

Buttermilk water-based eggshell paint

Large household paint brush

Metal ruler

Yellow ocher colored pencil

Decorator's tape

Window cleaner's squeegee, from which ½ inch wedges have been cut

Craft knife

Acrylic scumble glaze

Yellow ocher concentrated artist's acrylic

Dark ocher concentrated artist's acrylic

Square-ended artist's brush

Clear flat-finish acrylic varnish

Varnishing brush

preparation

Woodwork should be sanded, acrylic primer undercoat applied, and painted with 2 coats of buttermilk water-based eggshell paint

1 Mark squares

Divide each side of the sofa into squares, about 10 inches each (or as square as possible given the dimensions of the sofa). Using a pencil a similar color to the scumble, mark squares with the ruler.

2 Mask off squares

Using decorator's tape, mask off rows of alternate squares—these are the squares you will paint first. Put a piece of tape in the center of the squares to be painted later —this will prevent you from painting them inadvertently.

3 Paint squares

Tint the scumble to a desired depth of color with the yellow ocher paint. Using a large paint brush, apply the tinted scumble in long, even vertical brush strokes. You must not paint adjoining squares at the same time or the scumble will run.

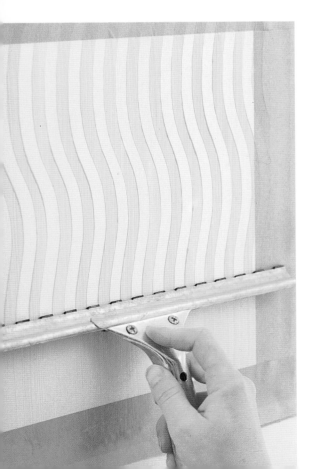 

4 Comb scumbled squares

For vertical wavy lines, start at the top of the square and drag the comb steadily through the tinted scumble to the bottom, moving the comb from side to side as you go. For even lines, it is best to drag the comb through the scumble in one fluid movement. Remove the tape and let it dry.

5 Vertical-lined squares

Repeat the masking, painting, and combing for all the vertical squares on alternate rows, remembering to mark center of the alternate squares with tape to paint the horizontal lines later. Remove the tape surrounding each finished square. Let it dry. Repeat for the remaining vertical squares on the sofa.

6 Horizontal-lined squares

Mask off the horizontal squares that do not touch along alternate rows. Remove the markers on the squares you have masked. Apply the tinted scumble, working on one square at a time as before, but this time with horizontal brush strokes. Drag the comb through the scumble as before, but this time up and down from left to right to create horizontal wavy lines. Remove the tape. Let it dry. Repeat the process for all the sides of the sofa for the first set of horizontal squares.

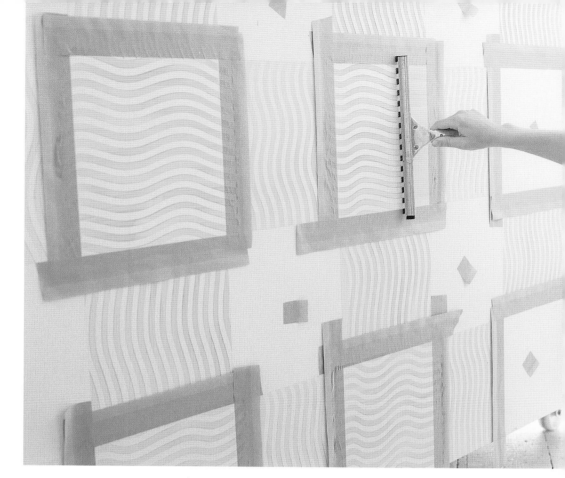

7 Alternating horizontals

Once the scumble has dried, mask off the remaining horizontal squares in the alternate rows. (Remove the marker tapes before painting.) Working on one square at at a time, apply the tinted scumble and create horizontal wavy lines as before. Repeat for each side of the sofa. Remove the decorator's tape. Let it dry.

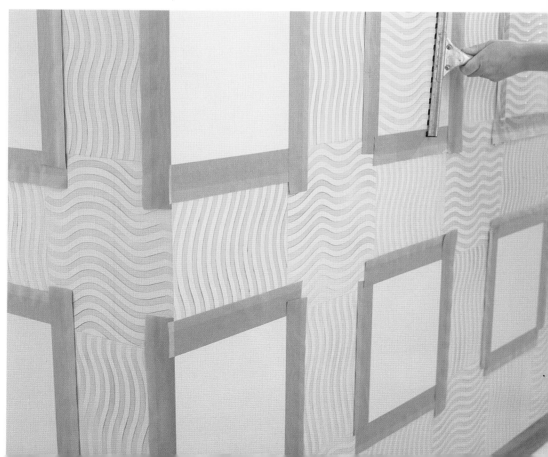

8 Paint edges of sofa

Using a square-ended artist's brush and
dark ocher, hand-paint the edges to give
the sofa a neat finish. Let it dry. Apply
2 coats of varnish to finish.

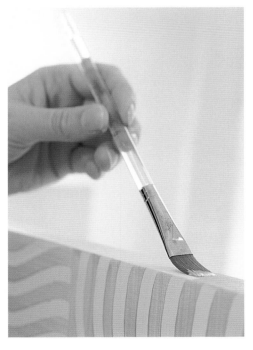

coffee table
broad stripes

materials

Wooden coffee table

Coarse- and fine-grit sandpaper

Masking tape

Large household paint brush

Concentrated artist's acrylic in light ocher and plum, diluted with water

Satin oil-based varnish

Varnishing brush

preparation

Table should be sanded—if the surface is rough, first sand it with coarse-grit sandpaper, then finish with fine-grit sandpaper

A coffee table is a useful piece of living-room furniture, which is given center stage in most homes, so style, size, shape, design, color, and material are all important. With this in mind, coffee tables make the perfect medium for painting and decorating. Colorwashing is an age-old technique that is as popular today as it has ever been. Its beauty lies in the subtle color treatment that allows the natural grain and textures of wood to show through and, for best results, should be used on soft wood or wood that has been sandblasted to absorb color.

Be sure to smooth the masking tape down well, to section off the panels; this will stop the color from one panel merging into another. Afterward, use a strong oil-based varnish to seal the wood.

Coffee tables can be heavy to move around, but attaching wheels to the legs overcomes this back-wrenching problem to become part of the table's overall modern appeal. If you wish, complement this contemporary setting with the up-to-the-minute combed sofa on page 32.

1 Section off panels with tape

Following the natural lines on the planks of wood that make up the table top, mask off 4 unequal panels; take the masking tape over the edge of the table.

2 Paint ocher acrylic panels

Using a large paint brush and diluted light ocher acrylic, fill in 2 alternate masked-off panels, remembering to paint over the edges of the table. Remove the tape. Let it dry.

3 Paint plum acrylic panels

Mask off the remaining alternate panels as before. Using a large paint brush and diluted plum acrylic, paint the panels on the top and edges of the table. Remove the tape. Let it dry. Apply 2 coats of varnish to finish.

large mirror
modern mosaic

materials

Wooden framed mirror

Decorator's tape

*Cream water-based
satinwood paint*

Household paint brush

Soft-lead pencil

Metal ruler

Plastic ruler

*Concentrated artist's acrylic in
light olive, umber, terracotta,
soft pink, and pale umber*

Square-ended artist's brush

Clear flat-finish acrylic varnish

Varnishing brush

preparation

*Frame of mirror should be
sanded; mirror masked off with
decorator's tape; acrylic primer
undercoat applied to frame
and painted with 2 coats of
cream water-based
satinwood paint*

This uncluttered room needs little besides a magnificent mosaic floor-standing mirror. Mosaic has a wonderfully timeless and peaceful appeal, especially when earth colors are used. The painted mirror looks like a labor of love, but only the accurate measuring and marking of the squares require serious attention. The painting itself is not as perfect as it first appears; in fact, the pattern benefits from the slightly imperfect or rough edges achieved from freehand painting. This is a project that can be worked on at your leisure—you could take two days from start to finish, or you could dip in and out of it as you might with sketching, knitting, or embroidery.

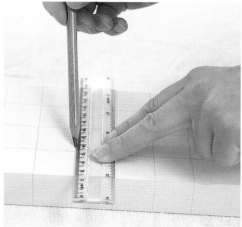

1 Draw lines along frame

Work out how many 1-inch squares you can fit in the frame of the mirror. (If the frame does not divide exactly, size the squares accordingly.) Using a pencil and ruler, draw parallel lines 1 inch apart from top to bottom and down the sides.

2 Finish squares

Once the parallel lines have been drawn in on all sides of the frame, add vertical lines 1 inch apart on all sides of the frame to complete the squares, remembering to take the pencil lines over the edge of the frame and down the sides.

3 Apply first color

Using a square-ended artist's brush and working with one color at a time, paint one square in every six light olive, taking the paint right up to the edge of the pencil lines. Don't forget to paint the outer and inner squares of the frame edge.

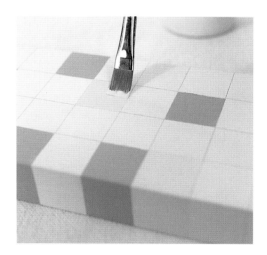

5 Complete squares

Continue to fill one square in every six, for the remaining three colors. Let the last set of squares dry. Apply 2 coats of varnish to finish.

4 Apply second color

Let the light olive squares dry before moving on to another color. Using soft pink paint and the same brush (which has been washed and dried), paint the next set of squares.

emphasize elegance with light

The faintest shade of yellow paint on this regal-looking mirror enhances and defines its delicate shape.

The linear design of this elegant wooden daybed brings furniture into a contemporary dimension. Checks do not seem to date, and when they are used for upholstery or slipcovers, they are always stylish and fresh.

colors

Pale, plain, and unobtrusive, this softly painted lamp base with a square cardboard shade does not dominate the small side table.

Kitchen furniture is ideal for painting—built-in cabinets, hutches, tables, and chairs take on a fresh look—even wooden floors can be given a new lease on life. Pattern ideas are taken from dishtowels, gingham fabric, and the more unusual floral print of a Japanese kimono.

cooking

and storing

storage cabinet
kimono flowers

materials

Wooden cabinet

*Red water-based
satinwood paint*

*Cream water-based
satinwood paint*

Household paint brushes

Self-adhesive stickers

Acetate

Black permanent marker pen

Craft knife

Cutting mat

*White conté pastel stick,
sharpened to a point*

Masking tape, low tack

*Dark red and cream
concentrated artist's acrylic*

Square-ended artist's brush

Fine-tipped artist's brush

Clear flat-finish acrylic varnish

Varnishing brush

preparation

*Cupboard should be sanded;
acrylic primer undercoat
applied; outside painted red,
inside and shelves painted
cream, using 2 coats of
water-based satinwood paint*

Storage is the key to an organized and practical kitchen, and this large open-front cabinet can hold a large number of dishes, glassware, and kitchenware. The inspiration for this stenciled floral pattern was an antique Japanese kimono—I took a small flower motif from a complex pattern and created a layered stencil (see template on page 124). The design is refreshingly simple, and painting flowers randomly on the outside of the cabinet not only breaks up the solid block of red, but gives the appearance of the flowers tumbling down the sides. The flowers are confined to the exterior of the cabinet only, to give the inside an uncluttered appearance. In an otherwise cream-colored kitchen, warm red adds a splash of color. The light interior of the cabinet gives the illusion of more space as well as complementing the cream china on the shelves. It is easy to create stencils from your own design or from other sources, and I have explained clearly on page 118 how this can be achieved.

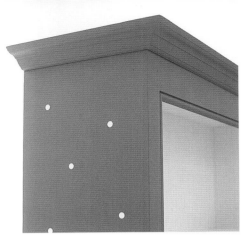

1 Mark position guides

Put self-adhesive stickers at random on both sides of the cabinet to mark the position for each flower. Copy the stencils (see page 124), scaling up or down as required. Trace onto acetate and include registration marks. Cut out using a craft knife and cutting mat.

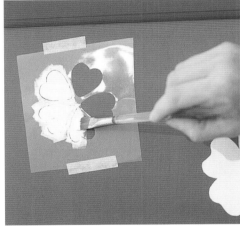

3 Paint in petaled stencil

Position the second stencil (the petaled flower) over a sticker, as for the first stencil, and paint in cream acrylic. Repeat, stenciling at random over several stickers on both sides of the cabinet. Wipe the stencil clean and use for the remaining stickers, this time painting in red acrylic. Let it dry.

2 Draw in registration marks

Tape the first stencil (the solid flower outline) over one sticker, then remove the sticker. Mark through the registration holes. Using a square-ended brush, fill in the stencil with cream acrylic. Lift off the stencil and repeat, stenciling in a random pattern over several stickers.

4 Stencil petals over flower

Put the second stencil (the petaled flower) over a solid cream flower, making sure the registration marks align with the original conté pastel marks. Fill in the stencil with red acrylic. Carefully remove stencil. Repeat, stenciling on top of the other solid cream flowers. Let it dry.

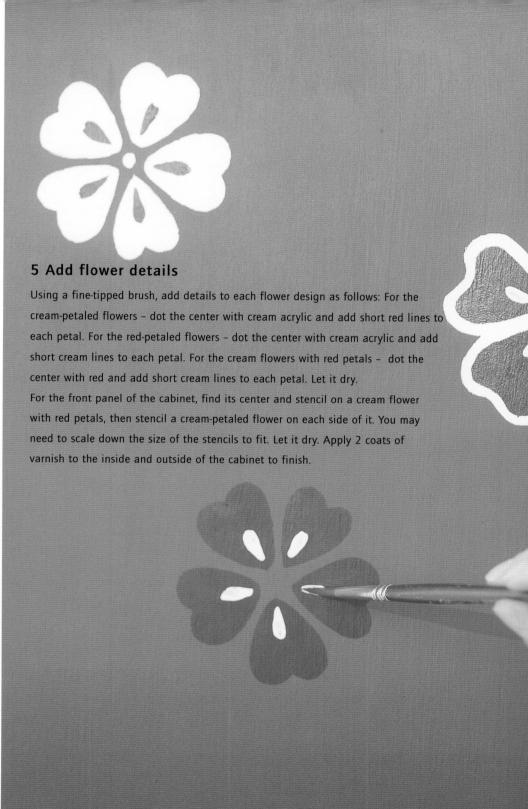

5 Add flower details

Using a fine-tipped brush, add details to each flower design as follows: For the cream-petaled flowers – dot the center with cream acrylic and add short red lines to each petal. For the red-petaled flowers – dot the center with cream acrylic and add short cream lines to each petal. For the cream flowers with red petals – dot the center with red and add short cream lines to each petal. Let it dry.

For the front panel of the cabinet, find its center and stencil on a cream flower with red petals, then stencil a cream-petaled flower on each side of it. You may need to scale down the size of the stencils to fit. Let it dry. Apply 2 coats of varnish to the inside and outside of the cabinet to finish.

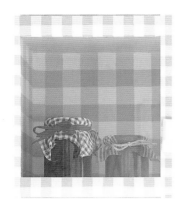

painted gingham

Gingham has such a timeless and fresh appeal that it is both naive and sophisticated. Interpreting it into a paint effect is most attractive. The checked pattern is created by the weaving of two colors; the third color is created where the two colors overlap. (Bear this in mind if you decide to use different colors.) As with all striped or checkerboard patterns, the key to success lies in the preparation and marking stage. Working out the size and scale of the pattern is important, but the ingenious use of a square-gridded stencil will facilitate painting. If you look closely at the squares that make up the finished pattern, you will see that they occasionally overlap a little. It is this slight overlap that gives the paint effect charm as well as the realistic appearance of fabric weave. The inside of the cabinet is stenciled in larger squares to provide a contrast to the outside. Also, it is less tricky to paint large squares within the confined space of a cabinet.

materials

Wooden glass-fronted wall cabinet

Decorator's tape

Water-based satinwood paint in light stone, ivory, and stone

Household paint brush

White conté pastel stick, sharpened to a point

Ruler

Masking tape, low tack

Graph paper

Black permanent marker pen

Acetate

Craft knife

Cutting mat

Spray adhesive

Square-ended artist's brush

Clear flat-finish acrylic varnish

Varnishing brush

preparation

Cabinet should be sanded, glass panes masked off with decorator's tape, acrylic primer undercoat applied, and painted with 2 coats of light stone water-based satinwood paint

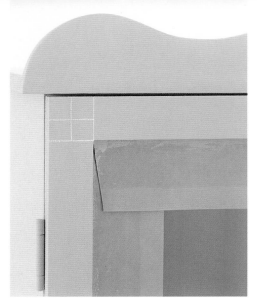 

1 Square off cabinet corners

Draw a square at each corner of the cabinet and on each side of each crossbar on the door, then divide into 4 smaller squares, about 1 inch each. This will make marking the rest of the cabinet more accurate. Join the large squares by drawing lines through the center of each one.

2 Make a marker tape

To make a marker tape for the squares, put a strip of masking tape down one side of the cabinet front. Using a ruler and pen, mark 1-inch intervals or intervals equivalent to the small squares already drawn at the corners. Use the tape and pastel to mark the front; join marks to form parallel lines.

3 Draw horizontal lines

Using the marker tape and conté pastel, make marks down both edges of one side of the cabinet. Draw in parallel lines, joining the marks, using a ruler for straight lines. Repeat the taping, marking, and joining process for the other side of the cabinet.

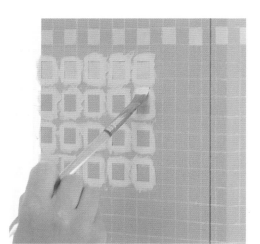  

7 Cover side with squares

Reposition the stencil, laying it on top of the grid, next to the first set of ivory squares and paint as before. Repeat on all the sides and front of the cabinet. Let it dry.

8 Stencil stone squares

For the gingham effect, use the same stencil as before, but this time start with the stencil 2 lines down from the top and 2 columns in from the edge. Paint the squares stone. Repeat stone pattern on all sides of cabinet.

9 Paint top row of squares

Mask off the row of ivory squares around the top of the cabinet and paint in a row of alternate gray squares. Using a household paint brush, paint the cornice stone. Remove masking and decorator's tape. Let it dry.

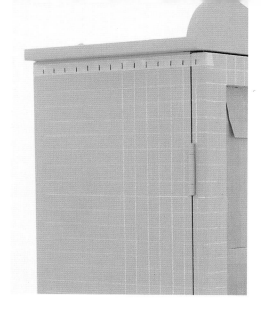

4 Draw vertical lines

Repeat the process for the vertical lines, but this time put the tape around the base of the cabinet and draw in marks. Do the same around the top, then join the marks from top to bottom to form a square grid.

5 Cut out a stencil of squares

On graph paper, draw a template of squares (the same size as the squares on the cabinet) and mark a cross in alternate squares on alternate rows. Tape acetate on top of the template. Using a craft knife and cutting mat, cut out the crossed squares.

6 Stencil cream squares

Apply spray adhesive to the back of the stencil and leave for 30 seconds until tacky. Starting one line down from the top, put the stencil on top of the grid over the first column of squares. Paint in the ivory squares, then carefully lift off the stencil.

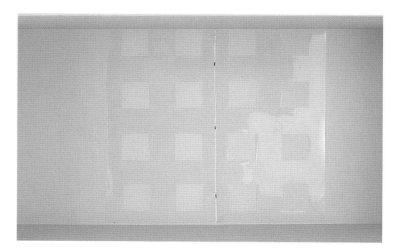

10 Find center inside cabinet

Make a larger square stencil, as before, and draw positioning marks down the center of the stencil. Find the center inside the cabinet and draw a vertical line to mark it. Secure the stencil in place, laying the positioning marks on top of the white line. Paint in ivory squares.

11 Stencil inside cabinet

Continue to stencil large cream squares around the inside walls of the cabinet, followed by large stone squares, using the same method as on the outside. Let it dry. Apply 2 coats of varnish, inside and outside, to finish.

kitchen table
dishtowel motif

materials

Polished steel-topped wooden table

Cream water-based satinwood paint

Household paint brushes

Decorator's tape

Black permanent marker pen

Drawing square or ruler

Red colored pencil

Masking tape, low tack

Yardstick

Acrylic scumble glaze

Red concentrated artist's acrylic

Flat oil-based varnish, extra pale

Varnishing brush

preparation

Table should be sanded, acrylic primer undercoat applied, and painted with 2 coats of cream water-based satinwood paint

Antique dishtowels come in an assortment of weaves and patterns. They may be elaborately stitched with embroidery or plainly decorated with a simple weave. Either way, they are immensely collectable. Based on the simple crossed lines of a traditional Irish linen dishtowel, a plain wooden work table with a practical polished-steel top is transformed into a fun, light, and airy piece of furniture that would blend into virtually any modern kitchen. Its chunky square legs, bottom shelf, and sides provide an ideal surface for a simple motif like this one. For the translucent paint effect that simulates the dishtowel weave, scumble glaze is used, mixed with artist's acrylic. To achieve the most effective look, keep the base color of the table white or ivory—the same as a dishtowel—and stay with the traditional colors of red and white, blue and white, or green and white.

1 Mark stripes on leg

Using a strip of decorator's tape the length of the table leg and a black pen, mark groups of 3 stripes (like dishtowel stripes) on the tape. Stick the marked tape on the edge of the table leg. Draw horizontal lines at the pen marks using a-square and red pencil.

2 Draw lines around leg

Remove the marker tape, then continue to draw the stripes around the table leg—butt the square against the side of the leg and make sure it lines up with the first set of red pencil lines. Repeat steps 1 and 2 for the other legs.

3 Mark front panel

Using the same marker tape as before and starting at one end of the table panel, make pencil marks to line up with the first group of lines at the top of the table leg. Continue to mark along the panel using the marker tape as a guide.

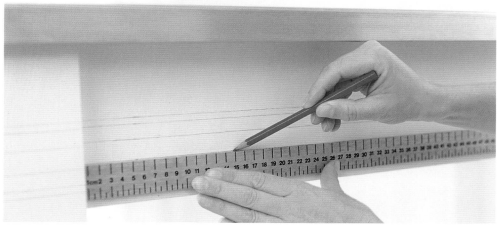

4 Draw parallel lines along front panel

Once all the marks have been made along the front panel, join them up. It is best to use a long ruler to join the marks to achieve perfect lines. Repeat steps 3 and 4 on the remaining panels of the table. If the table has a bottom shelf, measure, mark, and draw a group of horizontal lines along both lengths of it.

5 Mask off stripes

Using masking tape, mask off all the groups of horizontal stripes down the table legs, facing panels and bottom shelf. (Put the tape outside the pencil lines.)

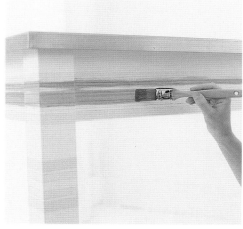

6 Paint red scumble lines

Tint the scumble glaze to a desired depth of color with red acrylic and paint in the masked-off areas. Direct the brush strokes in one direction for a streaked effect. Remove the tape. Dry, preferably overnight.

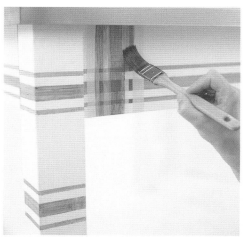

7 Cross-over lines

Mark, mask off, and paint cross-over lines as before. Remove tape. Let it dry. (Repeat for the bottom shelf so the cross-over lines match the panels.) Apply 2 coats of varnish.

serving tray
shaker bird

materials

Oval wooden tray, unvarnished

White conté pastel stick, sharpened to a point

Craft knife

Medium-sized potato

Square-ended artist's brush

Red concentrated artist's acrylic

Varnishing brush

Acrylic pickling paste

Lint-free cotton cloth

Fine steel wool (optional)

Flat oil-based varnish, extra pale

preparation

Tray should be clean, grease-free, and sanded with fine-grit sandpaper if neccessary

Pickling is a very old paint treatment that was originally used on woodwork to accentuate the woodgrain and to give a chalky finish. It has seen a revival in recent years as a paint finish because its appeal is so natural and pure. The simple repetition of a one-color motif works its own magic, particularly on small items such as this oval serving tray where the motif is the Shaker bird of peace. Potato printing is suprisingly easy and fun to do, and will probably remind you of childhood days when it was a favorite pastime.

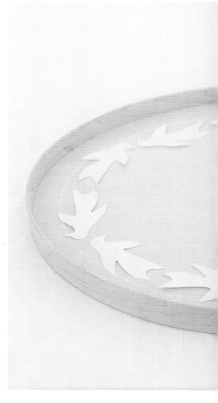

4 Apply pickling paste

Using a varnishing brush, paint a thin layer of pickling paste over the surface of the tray, covering the bird motifs as you go. You should still be able to see the bird design underneath.

1 Position bird cutouts

Using a conté pastel, mark a 2-inch border on the tray to represent the position guide for the cutouts. Make 12 copies of the shaker bird template (see page 122) and cut them out. Lay the birds in pairs, head-to-head around the tray on the inside of the border.

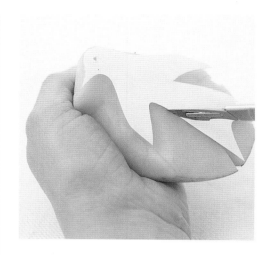

2 Cut around bird template

Cut a potato in half and press one bird cutout onto the wet surface of the cut potato to stick. Using a craft knife, cut away around the cutout to make a printing block, and using the tip of the knife, pierce a hole in the potato to make the bird's eye.

3 Print on tray surface

Dip the printing block into a saucer of red paint to coat. Remove a cutout from the tray and print a red bird in its place. Press the printing block firmly onto the tray, lift it off, and repeat for the remaining birds. (Recoat with paint as needed.) Let it dry.

5 Rub pickling paste into tray

Rub the tray all over with a soft, lint-free cotton cloth, working the cloth in a circular motion to achieve a bloomed effect. To give the tray a more distressed look, use steel wool to rub the surface. Apply 2 coats of varnish to finish. Let it dry.

add warmth with red painted

A whimsical triangular shelf, painted chalky white and red and hung by a thick rope, would not look out of place in a contemporary kitchen.

This rustic country-style egg rack is as practical as it is attractive; it has been varnished to withstand the rigors of kitchen life.

accessories

Old wooden spoon racks are a common antique shop or secondhand store find. The combination of straight and curved edges gives this three-tiered rack a unique appeal. The boldness of the red defines shape, making other forms of decoration unneccessary.

The bedroom is a haven we turn to for rest and tranquility, so choose blue tones of the sea and sky, paired with crisp shades of white—a classic combination—to evoke peace and calm. This chapter features vinegar painting and ragging, stenciling, and the delicate art of freehand painting.

rest and

sleep

materials

Wooden headboard

Pale blue latex paint

Household paint brush

Small self-adhesive stickers

Acetate

Black permanent marker pen

Craft knife

Cutting mat

Spray adhesive

Red concentrated artist's acrylic

Square-ended artist's brush

Clear flat-fiinish acrylic varnish

Varnishing brush

preparation

*Headboard should be
sanded, acrylic primer
undercoat applied, and
painted with 2 coats of pale
blue latex paint*

wooden headboard
heart motif

For centuries, hearts, like flowers, have been used symbolically to decorate painted furniture, embroidered textiles, and wood carvings. Hearts have such a nostalgic and romantic appeal that it is hardly suprising that they are as popular today as they have always been, and where more appropriate to feature them than in the bedroom.

The inspiration for the heart design on this wooden headboard comes from cross-stitch motifs found on antique bed and household linens. Traditionally motifs were embroidered in red yarns on white linen, so I have kept the red, but for a modern slant stenciled onto an ice-blue background instead of white. Red and blue are neighbors on the color spectrum, so they mix well together; but when used in conjunction with white, their brilliance seems to be heightened. Teaming crisp white bedlinen with this color scheme shows off the red hearts to their best. As the heart motif is geometric, care is needed when cutting out the stencil. Practice stenciling on another surface first.

1 Put stickers on headboard

To mark the position for the stencil, put self-adhesive stickers in a random pattern on the headboard. Make a copy of the heart template (see page 123), sizing it up or down as required. Trace onto acetate and cut out using a craft knife and cutting mat.

2 Spray stencil with adhesive

Lightly spray the back of stencil with spray adhesive and leave for 30 seconds until tacky. Position the center of the stencil, tacky side down, over one of the stickers. Press the stencil on to secure.

3 Paint hearts on headboard

Using a square-ended artist's brush, fill in the hearts with red acrylic. Carefully remove the stencil and repeat steps 1 and 2 for the remaining stickers on the headboard. Let it dry, then peel off the stickers. Apply 2 coats of varnish to finish.

country ragging

materials

Wooden bedside table

Masking tape, low tack

Vinegar paint (4 teaspoons cerulean blue powder paint and 1 teaspoon sugar dissolved in 1 tablespoon hot water, then mixed with ½ cup of vinegar and 1 cup warm water)

Large household paint brush

Thin plastic bag

Square-ended artist's brush

Tracing paper

Soft-lead pencil

Stencil board

Spray adhesive

Craft knife

Cutting mat

Ruler

White stencil paint

Flat oil-based varnish, extra pale

Varnishing brush

preparation

Table should be sanded, acrylic primer undercoat applied, and painted with 2 coats of white oil-based undercoat. Lightly sand again.

Vinegar painting is an early American wood-graining technique with a charm all its own, specially devised for speed in covering large areas. The effect is not always recognizable as wood graining, but more as a fanciful allover pattern. The vinegar keeps the paint slippery, so if you don't like the initial effect, you can simply wipe it off while it is still wet and start again. You can use many devices to apply the paint; I experimented and found that a thin plastic shopping bag, when crumpled up, worked exceptionally well. You could also try crumpled paper, modeling clay, or cloth rags. In general, a dark color painted over a light color works best, as seen here with this ragged bedside table: bright blue vinegar paint has been applied on top of a white base. Test a small area first with the vinegar paint, as you may experience cissing (where paint is unable to adhere to the surface and remains in tiny globules). If this happens, sponge the surface with whiting (see page 127), let it dry, dust off loose powder, and proceed as directed.

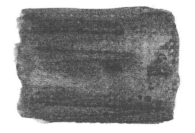

1 Apply vinegar paint to side panel

The painting has to be done in stages or the paint will dry before you have the chance to create the crumpled effect. Mask off the top edge of table all the way around and the inside edges of the legs (these edges will be painted last). Using a large brush, apply the vinegar paint with crisscross brush strokes.

2 Crumple painted surface

Crumble a plastic bag into a sausage shape. Dab it over the surface of the paint on the side panel before it dries. Use different parts of the bag for a varied effect and dab randomly. Repeat the painting and dabbing on the remaining side panels and top of the table. Carefully peel off the tape. Let it dry.

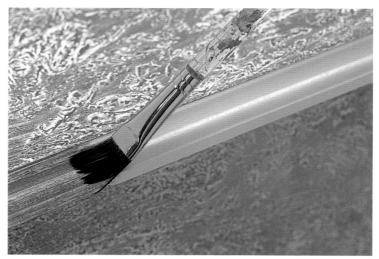

3 Dab top inside edge of table legs

Carefully paint and dab the four legs the same way, making sure you dab the crumpled plastic bag into the corners and inside edge for an even, overall appearance. Let it dry.

4 Paint top edge of table

Using a square-ended artist's brush, paint the edge around the table with the vinegar paint. While the paint is still wet, dab with the crumpled plastic bag as before. Let it dry.

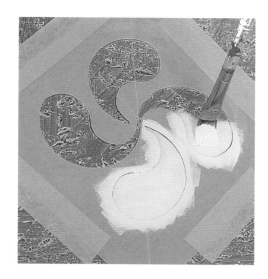

5 Stencil swirl motif

Trace the swirl motif (see page 123) onto tracing paper, stick onto stencil board with spray adhesive. and cut out with a craft knife and cutting mat. Find the center of one side panel and draw a cross to mark it. Using strips of masking tape, anchor the stencil in place, making sure its center goes over the cross. Fill in the stencil with white paint. Remove the stencil. Join the segments of the swirl by painting the gap where they meet. Let it dry and apply 2 coats of varnish to finish.

storage trunk
simple initials

materials

Wooden trunk

Water-based satinwood paint in tan, pale blue, and stone

Household paint brushes

Ruler

Soft-lead pencil

Masking tape, low tack

Tracing paper

Square-ended artist's brush

Fine-tipped artist's brush

Clear flat-finish acrylic varnish

Varnishing brush

preparation

Trunk should be sanded, acrylic primer undercoat applied, and painted with 2 coats of tan water-based satinwood paint

A personalized storage trunk would make a lovely gift for a wedding, a christening, or a special anniversary. There is something unique about having your own initials and a commemerative date painted onto a chest or trunk. There are many old painted chests in museums and antique shops, some richly decorated with beautiful designs and original motifs—these are wonderful sources of inspiration—and you could copy these designs or create your own. The trunk has a very modern feel to it; its beauty lies in its simplicity decorated as it is with a plain, wide band of color onto which oversized letters and numbers are painted. I have included a template of a plain yet attractive alphabet and numerals for you to copy (see pages 74–77), scaling up or down on a photocopier to fit the trunk or chest. Don't feel bound to using the same tan, pale blue, and stone colors suggested here, but rather choose tones and shades that tie in to and compliment the existing color scheme in your bedroom or guest room.

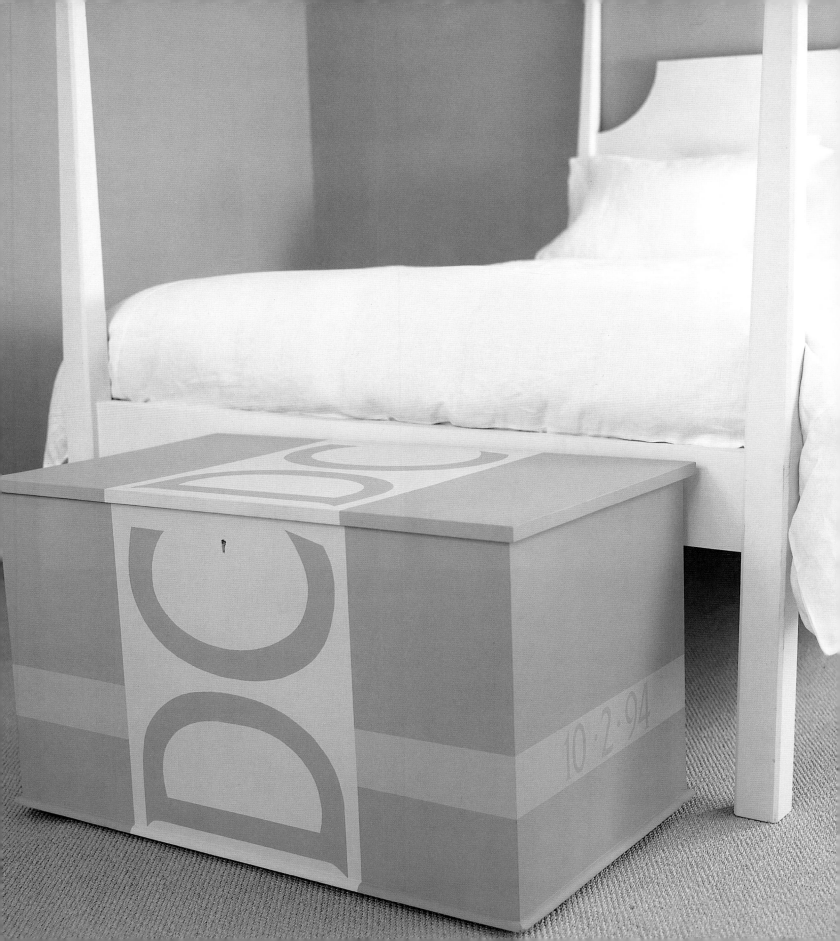

1 Mask off panels on top of trunk

Using a ruler and pencil, measure and mark 3 panels on top of the trunk (the center panel should be about 1½ times the width of the 2 outer panels) and mask off with masking tape. Using fingers, smooth down the tape to prevent paint from seeping underneath.

2 Paint outer panels blue

Using a household brush, paint the outer panels pale blue. Remove the tape. Draw panels on the front and back of the trunk to line up with the panels on top. Mask off and paint blue, as before. Remove the tape. Paint both ends of the trunk pale blue and let it dry.

3 Paint a stone band around the trunk

Using a ruler and pencil, mark and draw a band around the blue panels near the base of the trunk. Mask off outside the pencil lines. Paint the band with stone paint. Remove the tape. Let it dry.

4 Trace letters from template

Photocopy 2 letters from this page, large enough to fit in the center panel on top of the trunk, and cut them out. Lay the first letter in position, tape tracing paper over it, and trace the outline. Repeat for the second letter, on the same tracing paper, making sure the letters are equally spaced.

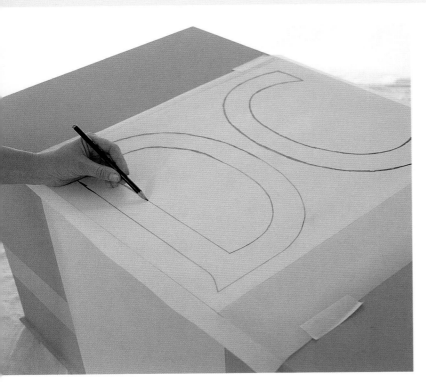

5 Transfer image of letters to trunk top

Take the tracing paper off, reverse it so the letters appear back to front and using a pencil, go over the lines. Reverse the tracing paper again and tape it in position on the trunk top. Draw over the outline to transfer the letters to the panel. Remove the tracing paper. Draw over any faint lines. Repeat lettering on the front panel of the trunk.

6 Paint letters pale blue

Using a small, square-ended artist's brush, fill in the letters on the top and front of the trunk with the same pale blue paint as before. If your hand is not too steady, it may be helpful to mask off any straight edges of the letters before painting them.

W X Y Z

7 Paint numbers for date

Repeat the tracing and transferring steps for the date, to fit in the stone band on the side of the trunk—the middle number should be in the center of the band. Using a fine-tipped brush, fill in with the same pale blue paint as before, painting over the pencil lines. Let it dry.

8 An important date

Repeat the date in the stone band on the other side of the trunk, making sure the numbers and dots are evenly spaced, as before. Let it dry. Apply 2 coats of varnish to finish.

6 7 8 9 0

friendship box
crested garland

materials

Wooden box

Concentrated artist's acrylic in pale blue, dark blue, and indigo

Household paint brush

Black permanent marker pen

Ruler

White conté pencil, sharpened

Masking tape, low tack

White Plaka paint

Square-ended artist's brush

Tracing paper

Soft-lead pencil

Fine-tipped artist's brush

Clear flat-finish acrylic varnish

Varnishing brush

preparation

Box should be sanded, acrylic primer undercoat applied, and painted with 2 coats of pale blue concentrated artist's acrylic

Small wooden boxes have endless possibilities for storage—jewelry, family photographs, important papers and documents, sewing kit or even as a place to put odds and ends. A medium-sized wooden box with a hinged lid is best for this project. Here, I have painted the box with narrow blue stripes and then decorated the top with a dotted outline of a heart, enclosed by a delicate garland of white leaves and simple flowers. The combination of blues looks sophisticated, and the white garland adds charm and elegance. Don't be deterred by the number of steps involved in painting and decorating this box—it may seem complicated, but the steps follow a systematic and logical order—the important thing to remember here is the sequence of taping and then painting the stripes. I have recommended concentrated artist's acrylic for the stripes. Alternatively, you could use small tester pots of household paints, available from hardware stores. The opaqueness of Plaka paint, for the garland, is perfect for painting over strong blues.

1 Draw lines on box top

Make pen marks at equal intervals along both lengths of the lid and continue down each side of the box. Using a conté pencil and ruler, mark a central panel on the lid.

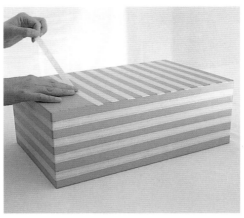

2 Put masking tape on box

Mask off stripes on the lid and around the sides of the box. Using fingers, smooth down the masking tape to prevent paint from seeping underneath.

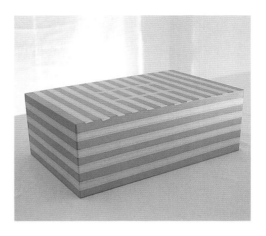

3 Mask off central panel

Put a strip of masking tape on the 2 long sides of the central panel on the lid, making sure the tape is on the inside of the white conté pencil line.

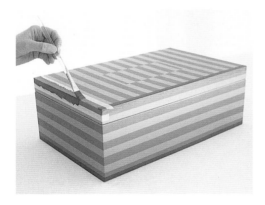

7 Edge box with a border

To make the border, put strips of masking tape around the base of the box, ¾ inch up from the bottom, and paint an indigo border. Remove the tape. Let it dry. Do the same for all the outside edges of the box top, lid, and sides.

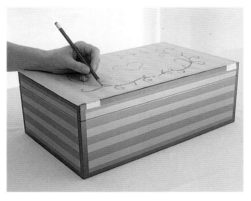

8 Transfer image onto box top

Enlarge the heart and garland motif (see page 120) on a photocopier and trace onto tracing paper. (Draw registration marks to match up with the corners of the panel so the heart is central in the panel.) Tape the tracing paper face down onto the box and outline the design in pencil. Remove the tracing and carefully go over the outline.

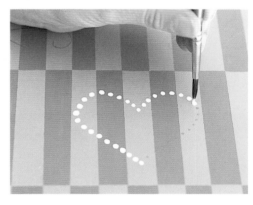

9 Paint a dotted outline

Using a fine-tipped artist's brush, lightly dot white paint over the pencil marks of the heart motif on the box top. Let it dry.

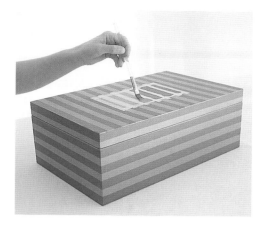

4 Paint masked-off box blue

Using a square-ended brush, paint dark blue stripes on the top and sides of the box, going over the masking tape slightly, but taking care not to paint over the central panel. Remove the tape. Let it dry.

5 Mask off central panel

Mask off the central panel by lining up strips of tape with the dark blue stripes on top of the box. Put masking tape all around the outside of the white line for the central panel. Smooth down the tape as before.

6 Paint striped panel

Paint dark blue stripes in the central panel, painting between the strips of masking tape. Remove the tape. Let it dry.

10 Add flower details

For the stems, paint white lines over the pencil marks, add leaves, and dot in the flowerheads. For the petals, lightly fill the artist's brush with white paint and press the brush down into postion, twist it, and lift off immediately to reveal petal shapes. Let it dry, then finish with 2 coats of varnish.

contemporary style in classic

A treasured photograph of a loved one can take pride of place in a specially decorated frame. This wooden frame has been painted with pale blue and pure white checks, then lightly pickled to mute the colors.

These bright blue antique chairs, through years of wear and tear, manage to hold an impressive stance with their high straight backs in a totally white room.

blue and white

The intricate fretwork of this white painted shelf is shown off in sharp detail when set against the vivid blue of the wall. An antique ceramic pot adds a happy note as it sits quietly on the shelf.

The bathroom has a dual purpose: a place for cleansing and a sanctuary for relaxation. A harmonious ambience is needed, so the warming tones of pink are called for. This chapter describes how to crackle glaze a stool and add a burst of sunray to a shelf and symmetry to a peg rail.

simple

bathing

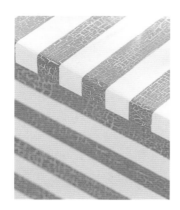

bath stool
beach stripes

A wooden stool makes a good resting place to pile soft towels, soaps, and shampoo while you soak away the hours and relax in a steaming hot bath. The stool can also be a temporary or permanent piece of bathroom furniture. Traditionally, crackle glaze is used to give furniture a distressed, aged look, but here the pattern created by the cracked surface is used to create a contemporary look. The glaze is applied on top of a light color and sandwiched by a dark color. Then, as the top coat of paint dries and contracts the light color shows through the cracks. The technique itself is simple, but for successful results instructions must be followed carefully. Apply crackle glaze evenly, directing brush strokes one way, and let the glaze dry thoroughly before painting over it. Humidity, temperature, and the type of surface can affect crackle glaze, so it is best to experiment on a similar surface before embarking on this project; aim for soft, subtle, and even cracks.

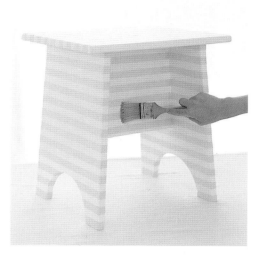

1 Mark stripes

Using a pink colored pencil and ruler, mark intervals the width of the masking tape along the 2 short lengths of the stool top. Repeat for the inner and outer sides of the stool.

2 Mask off stripes

Mask off stripes using the pink pencil marks as a guideline. To prevent paint from seeping under the tape, rub fingers over the tape next to the area to be painted.

3 Apply crackle glaze

If you have not used crackle glaze before, practice on another surface first. Using a flat brush and taking brush strokes in one direction only, apply the crackle glaze over the stool. Let it dry.

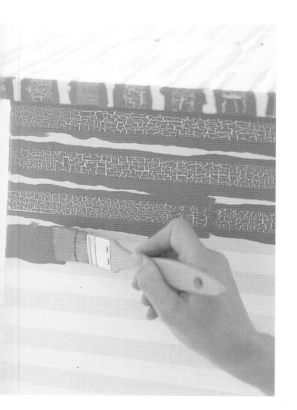

4 Paint pink stripes

Using a flat brush, apply the pink paint over the dried crackle glaze. When painting, take care not to brush over the area already painted or the crackled effect may spoil. The painted surface will begin to crack within seconds. Let it dry.

5 Remove masking tape

Carefully peel the masking tape away from the painted edges to reveal crackled pink stripes. Apply 2 coats of varnish to finish.

peg rail shelf
sunburst design

materials

Wooden shelf unit

Pale pink water-based
satinwood paint

Pink and dark pink
concentrated artist's acrylic

Household paint brush

Tracing paper

Soft-lead pencil

Masking tape, low tack

Square-ended artist's brush

Flat oil-based varnish, extra pale

Varnishing brush

preparation

Shelf should be sanded, acrylic
primer undercoat applied, and
painted with 2 coats of pale
pink satinwood paint

A splash of sunburst in chalky pinks brightens this pretty hanging shelf, providing practical storage for bathroom accessories and beauty and cleansing products, as well as being a striking piece of painted furniture. A novel method of attaching the shelf to the wall—simply hung from pegs—introduces another element of interest to the overall Shaker-look. The sunburst motif was adapted from a pattern taken from an old elaborately decorated patchwork quilt. I was struck by the sharp lines and geometric dimensions, which seem to have an almost 3-D effect. You don't have to restrict yourself to decorating a shelf, as this versatile design would be equally stunning painted directly onto the wall or in the middle of a wooden floor. Care is needed to trace the motif accurately and to position it centrally on the shelf. Be sure to mask off pencil lines exactly with tape, so each individual triangle and diamond, that forms the sunburst, is truly symmetrical.

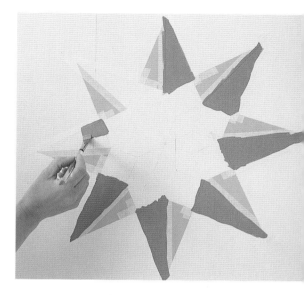

1 Transfer image to shelf back

Make a copy of the sunburst motif (see page 122), sizing it up or down on a photocopier. Trace onto tracing paper and tape it onto the shelf with the pencil lines face down. Using a pencil, draw over the design to transfer the image onto the shelf. Remove the tracing paper and go over the pencil outline with a pencil if the lines are faint.

2 Paint alternate triangles

Mask off alternate triangles around the outside of the sunburst, making sure the strips of masking tape are outside the pencil line. Using fingers, smooth down the tape to prevent paint from seeping underneath. Using a square-ended brush, fill in each masked-off triangle with 2 coats of pink paint. Remove the tape. Let it dry.

3 Paint dark pink triangles

Repeat step 2 for the remaining triangles around the outside of the sunburst and fill in with 2 coats of dark pink paint. Remove the tape. Let it dry.

5 Paint dark pink diamonds

Repeat step 4 for the remaining diamonds, filling in with dark pink. Let it dry. Apply 2 coats of varnish to finish.

4 Paint diamond shapes

To mask and paint the diamond shapes in the middle of the sunburst, you will need to work on one at a time. Put strips of masking tape around the outside of one diamond shape, smooth down the tape, and paint in pink. Remove the masking tape and let it dry. Repeat the process for the remaining alternate diamond shapes. Let it dry.

materials

Wooden peg rail

Dark rose water-based satinwood paint

Household paint brush

Ruler

White conté pastel stick, sharpened to a point

Tracing paper

Soft-lead pencil

Masking tape, low tack

Cream and brown concentrated artist's acrylic

Square-ended artist's brush

Fine-tipped artist's brush

Clear flat-finish acrylic varnish

Varnishing brush

preparation

Peg rail should be sanded, acrylic primer undercoat applied, and painted with 2 coats of dark rose water-based satinwood paint

peg rail
roman numerals

The simplest ideas are often the most impressive. Keeping this peg rail plainly decorated, uncluttered by pattern or embellishment, ties in well with the simple style associated with the Shakers. Also, in keeping with the Shaker ethos of functionalism, this peg rail can be useful for hanging damp towels to dry. Soft fluffy towels that have been appliquéd with matching numerals are an added feature. The symmetrical lines of the numerals above each peg is pleasing to the eye, and a sense of order can be felt by numbering an object—it is also a fun way to identify one's peg in a large family or in a clockroom at school. You don't have to limit this design to peg rails, you could also paint numerals onto chairs, or bedroom doors—a tradition still seen today in Swedish manor houses. Photocopy the numerals from the template on pages 96–97, sizing them up or down as necessary, then trace and transfer onto the peg rail. Outlining the numerals in brown defines shape and enhances the finish.

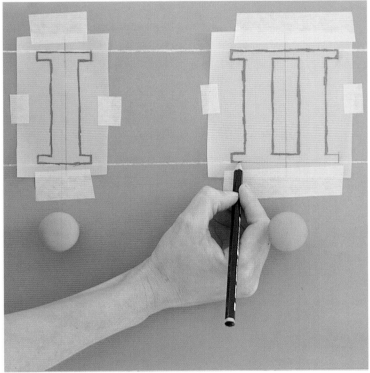

1 Measure and mark panels on peg rail

Make a copy of the numerals on this page, enlarge on a photocopier, and trace onto tracing paper. Using a ruler and conté pastel, mark a panel on the peg rail. (The width of the panel should be the same as the height of the traced numerals.) At each peg, draw a vertical line through the panel to mark the postion line for each numeral.

2 Transfer motifs onto peg rail

Using the vertical lines above each peg as a guide, tape the tracing paper into position, making sure the pencil outline is face down on the peg rail. Retrace the lines. Remove the tracing paper and using a pencil, carefully go over any unclear pencil lines.

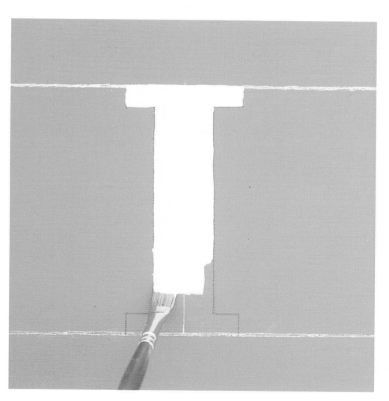

3 Paint numerals cream

Using a small square-ended artist's brush and working inside the pencil line, paint the numerals cream—the edges of each numeral when painted freehand will not be perfectly straight. Let it dry. If neccessary, apply another coat of cream paint to the numerals. Let it dry.

4 Paint a brown border around numerals

Outline the numerals in brown: paint a border around each one. Let it dry. Go over the border again in brown paint to create a bold outline. Don't worry if the outline is not perfectly straight, as this gives character to the peg rail. Rub out the conté pastel lines. Apply 2 coats of varnish to finish.

white-on-white for freshness

In a pure white setting, carved woodwork will add visual interest and dimension.

A white-on-white interior always strikes an impressive chord in a bathroom where cleanliness is of paramount importance.

Assorted wooden containers are brought to life with the slightest dash of red.

An exquisitely crafted wooden panel stands guard in front of a less than attractive radiator. It doesn't obscure heat from the room; it can filter through the dainty cutouts of the stylized flower design.

A traditional Shaker mirror is painted white, bringing it in line with the contemporary look of today.

A hall creates the first impression for visitors to your home, so plan its style and color scheme carefully. A theme, such as a woodland, using cool greens and aquas will invite your guests to feel welcome. Here, ferns have been silhouetted onto a table, and several storage boxes have been stenciled with leaves.

halls and

entrances

hall table
forest fern

materials

Round wooden table

Pale olive water-based eggshell paint

Household paint brush

Fresh sprigs of fern

Spray adhesive

Can of artist's blue spray paint

Flat oil-based varnish, extra pale

Varnishing brush

preparation

Table should be sanded, acrylic primer unercoat applied, and painted with 2 coats of pale olive water-based eggshell paint

The appeal of motifs drawn from nature is universal, whether it is flowers, leaves, or grasses. Their attractive shapes are easy to transfer into pattern and look comfortable in a contemporary setting. Country woodlands and city parks are filled with the heady scent of fern and bracken, and their uniquely shaped delicate fronds make an ideal template for a modern paint effect, which is so easy to achieve. All you need to do is gather sprigs of fern and stick them down in a pleasing arrangement onto the table, then simply spray canned paint evenly over the top until it is covered. Canned spray paints are available in a wide colour range from good art supply stores. Once the paint has dried, peeling the ferns off the table is incredibly satisfying, and as your pattern slowly emerges, the slightly imperfect and fuzzy edges of the fern silhoutte looks enchanting. For dramatic impact, this paint effect works best as a dark color sprayed on top of a light color—the finished effect is quite ethereal!

1 Select sprigs of fern for table

Lay the fern on a flat surface so you can choose sprigs that are a
good shape, flat, and healthy. Include in your selection ferns of
different sizes.

2 Apply spray adhesive to back of fern sprigs

Arrange the fern in a random pattern on the table top and edge.
Remove one sprig of fern at a time, spray the back with adhesive
away from the table and stick in place on the table as planned.

3 Press fern on table

Using the palms of your hands,
press the fern sprigs down
so they are stuck as flat as
possible onto the table top and
edge. You may find that the
thick stems of the large sprigs
do not stick well to the table—
don't worry if this happens; the
result will still be successful.

4 Apply spray paint

Following the instructions on the can of
spray paint, spray the fern-covered table.
Make sure you spray evenly over the entire
surface of the table. Let it dry.

5 Remove fern sprigs

Lift off the sprigs to reveal fern imprints.
Dust off any loose bits of fern. Apply
2 coats of varnish to finish.

stacking boxes
modern leaves

A stack of assorted plain cardboard boxes can be impressively transformed into objects of desire, using a wonderful combination of colors and simple leaf patterns. Here, each box has a different leaf stenciled on top of a vivid base color and then simple veins lightly painted in. You can choose to copy the oak leaf, chestnut leaf, or the branching leaves (see templates on pages 124-125), or pick out your favorite leaf design or botanical image from which to create a stencil. Tester pots of latex paint, available from hardware stores, are great value for small-scale projects such as this one. These delightful designs can also be used to decorate small chests or trunks. For a festive treat, present your gifts in boxes that have been painted in Christmas colors and decorated with holly or mistletoe.

1 Paint oak leaf stencil

Make a copy of 2 oak leaves (see page 124) on acetate and using a craft knife and cutting mat, cut them out. Spray the back of the large leaf stencil with spray adhesive and leave until tacky. Lay the stencil, tacky side down, slightly off center on the lid. Using a square-ended brush, fill in with turquoise paint. Repeat over the box lid.

2 Stencil side of box lid

To take the leaf design over the top edge of the box, put the stencil partway over the top of the lid and fill it in. Lift the stencil off and lay it flat against the side of the box lid, lining up the edges of the stencil with the painted leaf on top. Fill in the stencil to complete the leaf design. Repeat steps 1 and 2 until the lid is covered in leaves.

3 Complete leaves near top

Remove the lid and turn the box on its side. Reposition the large leaf stencil over any incomplete leaves near the top edge of the box and fill in. Repeat steps 1 and 2 for the other sides. Let it dry. Stencil in small leaf designs to fill the gaps between the large leaves on the lid and sides of the box.

1 Draw branch and stems

For the branch, draw a white pastel line slightly off center from corner to corner on the box top. For the stems, draw lines at right angles to the branch line and continue the lines down the sides of the box.

2 Paint branch and stems

Using a fine-tipped artist's brush and cream paint, add fine lines over the white pastel lines to cover. Let it dry.

3 Add leaves to stem lines

To paint the leaves, work on one side of the stem line at a time. Load the brush with cream paint and press it into position at the start of a stem. To form the leaf shape, as you pull back the brush, twist it off. Repeat along both sides of each stem. Let it dry.

4 Paint leaf veins

Using a fine-tipped artist's brush and the same lime-green as the box, paint in the leaf veins. Let it dry, then apply 1 coat of varnish to finish.

4 Paint leaf veins

Using a fine-tipped artist's brush and the same turquoise paint as the box, paint in the leaf veins. Let it dry. Apply 1 coat of varnish to finish.

define shape with color

A simple yet elegant wooden cabinet blends well into the background. Its cool color brings freshness and sublty to a hall, creating a welcoming atmosphere to carry throughout the house.

Neutral colors work particulary well. Here à delicate shade of beige allows the items on display in this small cupboard to be the focal point.

The unusual shape of this upright country settle adds to its simple charm. Seafoam green woodwork accentuates the sharp outline against the white wall. A gingham blue squab and bolster give a softer feel.

Pick furniture with clean lines and interesting features. Although verging on the puritanical, this bench sits comfortably on a terracotta tiled floor.

basic techniques

Following a few basic guidelines will help you to achieve paint effects that have a professional look:

Use the correct tools for the job You needn't buy much specialized equipment; more often than not, you can use good-quality household paint brushes. You will only need two or three different sizes of artist's brushes, so it is worth investing in good-quality ones that will not lose their bristles. Other essential tools are a sharp craft knife, ruler, low-tack masking tape, permanent marker pen, white conté pastel stick or pencil, and acetate sheets for stencils.

Prepare the surface All wooden surfaces should be sanded with sandpaper, dusted with a soft brush, wiped clean with a damp cloth, and then left to dry. Wood is porous, and to prevent paint from penetrating into it, must be primed. In most cases, I have recommended using an acrylic primer undercoat, which is water-based and quick drying. Apply one coat of primer and let it to dry thoroughly before painting on top with eggshell or satinwood paint. In general, a piece of furniture should receive two coats of paint, but you could get away with only one if the piece of furniture is not intended for heavy use.

Finishing a piece is as important as its preparation All painted surfaces benefit from being varnished to seal and protect the paint effect.

Finally, a good rule to follow with any paint technique is: practice on another surface first.

paints, glazes, and varnishes

Paints have improved greatly over recent years, resulting in new-generation paints that are ecologically friendly and easy and safe to use. For simplicity, most of the projects in this book have been worked in a combination of four types of water-based paint: ideal for wood since it allows the wood to "breathe."

Water-based eggshell paint A quick-drying paint with an almost flat finish, specially formulated for use on wooden surfaces. Available in a huge color choice in standard sizes.

Water-based satinwood paint A quick-drying paint with a low-sheen finish, specially formulated for use on wooden surfaces. Available in a large color palette. Available in small quantities, ideal for use on small projects.

If you wish, eggshell and satinwood paint can be used interchangeably.

Concentrated artist's acrylic Good color selection in small sizes available from art supply stores. They can be mixed with other acrylics or glazes, and can be thinned with water, making them ideal for freehand painting and stenciling.

Plaka paint An opaque, traditional casein flat-finish paint, available in small sizes from art supply stores. Used for painting decorative details.

Powder paints can be diluted with water and used in vinegar painting. Water-based acrylic glazes are readily available and used to create broken colorwork: scumble glaze, colored with acrylic paint, produces a textured effect that is ideal for stippling, combing, and ragging; crackle glaze is used to give a painted surface a cracked effect. Oil-based glazes are slow drying: they keep the paint "open" longer to create patterns in it.

Varnishes are essential for sealing and protecting painted surfaces. The most commonly used are oil-based and water-based, and both are available in flat, satin, or gloss finishes. An oil-based varnish is very hard-wearing, which makes it suitable for bathroom and dining furniture. However, it has a slight yellow tinge that can darken painted surfaces, so, where appropriate, I have suggested an extra-pale, flat, oil-based varnish instead. In most cases I have recommended clear flat-finish acrylic varnish because it is colorless, easy to apply, quick drying, and does not yellow with age. It also has a tough finish. While it is possible to apply an oil-based varnish over a water-based paint, it is not advisable to apply a water-based varnish over an oil-based paint.

brushes

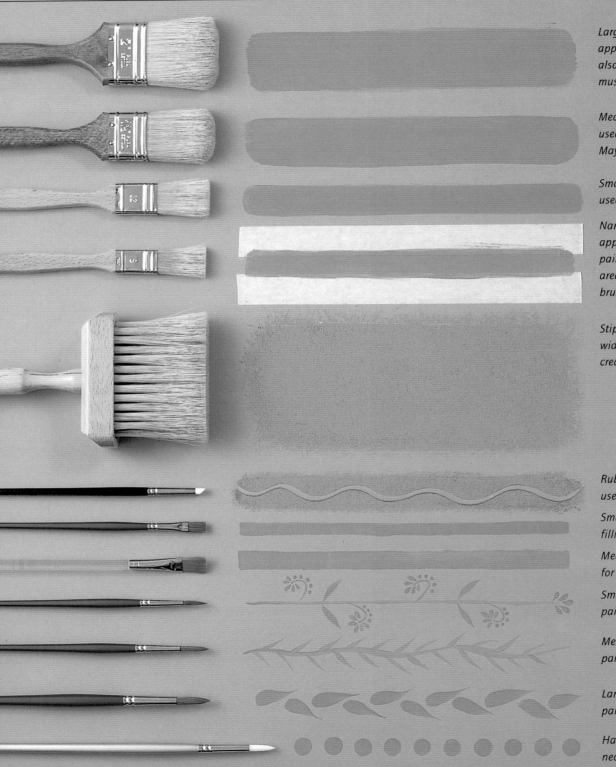

Large household paint brush used for applying paint over a large area. May also be used as a varnishing brush, but must be kept for this purpose only.

Medium-size household paint brush used for applying paint over surfaces. May also be used as a varnishing brush.

Small household paint brush. May also be used as a varnishing brush.

Narrow household paint brush used for applying paint over small areas, or for painting thin strips between masked-off areas. May also be used as a varnishing brush, but kept for this purpose only.

Stippling brush or dusting brush. A wide brush with soft bristles ideal for creating a stippled paint effect.

Rubber-ended brush with a wedged tip used to create patterns in wet paint.

Small square-ended artist's brush used for filling in stencils.

Medium square-ended artist's brush used for filling in stencils.

Small fine-tipped artist's brush used for painting fine lines and details.

Medium fine-tipped artist's brush used for painting fine lines and details.

Large fine-tipped artist's brush used for painting fine lines, shapes, and leaves.

Hard-tipped artist's brush for painting neat circles and dots.

drawing tools and stamps

Soft-lead pencil ideal for tracing and transfering motifs.

Colored pencil used for marking painted surfaces in a similar color.

White conté pencil used for marking surfaces.

Conté pastel stick used as an alternative to a conté pencil, for marking guidelines and registration marks.

Potato used for making a printing block. Can be dipped into paint or paint can be applied to the surface with a paint brush. Recoat the block with paint as needed.

Sponge roller refill used for making a stamping tool for a simple motif and used to stamp a repeating pattern.

Window cleaner's squeegee. "Teeth" are cut out from the rubber part to create a combing tool that is dragged through a tinted scumble glaze to create wavy lines, zigzags, or swirls.

making a stencil

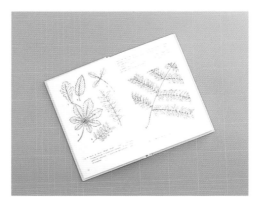

1 Choose an image to copy

A simple design motif is the best choice from which to create a template, so choose an image that will be easy to copy. Images can be taken and adapted from many sources including fabric, books, or magazines.

2 Copy image to scale

Using a photocopier, scale the image up or down to fit the area you want to stencil. For a large template, it may be necessary to first enlarge the image on a photocopier, then enlarge the enlargement.

3 Trace stencil from image

Tape tracing paper over the photocopy. Using a pencil, convert the image into a stencil enclosing areas within a continuous line. Remove the tracing of the template and tape onto a cutting mat.

5 Fill in stencil with paint

Using masking tape or spray adhesive, secure the stencil in place. Fill in using a square-ended artitst's brush and opaque paint such as concentrated artist's acrylic or stencil paint. (You may need to apply 2 coats of paint.) Remove the stencil and let it dry.

4 Cut out stencil

Tape acetate over the stencil template, and using a permenant marker pen, trace the image. Using the tip of a sharp craft knife, cut on the pen line to remove pieces of acetate to create a stencil.

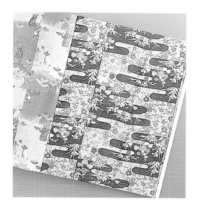

1 Select an image

To create a layered stencil from a complex design, pick out a specific detail such as a flower motif to copy and simplify.

2 Scale image to size

Scale the flower motif up or down on a photocopier. Make a freehand drawing of the scaled motif from which to copy.

3 Draw freehand

Using a compass and pencil, draw a circle (the size of the image) on paper and divide into 5 equal sections. Copy the petal design in each section. Draw in registration marks.

4 Make two stencils

Tape acetate over the template and using a permanent pen, trace the 5 individual inner parts and the registration marks. Repeat for the second stencil, this time tracing outline.

5 Cut out stencils

Using a sharp craft knife and a cutting mat, cut out the two stencils following the pen lines. Remove and discard the cutout pieces of acetate. Cut out the registration marks.

6 Paint one stencil

Tape or spray glue the stencil of the flower outline into place and draw in registration marks. Using a square-ended brush, fill in the stencil with one color. Remove stencil and let it dry.

7 Stencil petals over stenciled outline

Secure the petaled stencil, as before, on top of the stenciled flower outline, aligning the registration marks. Fill in the stencil with a different color. (You may need 2 coats of paint.) Remove the stencil and let it dry.

suppliers

paint suppliers and art material suppliers

Art Supply Warehouse Express
5325 Departure Drive
Railegh, NC 27604
Fine artist's supplies. Mail
order. Catalog.

Benjamin Moore Paints
Montvale, New Jersey
New York, NY
Period-style paints in
muted shades.

Charrette
31 Olympia Avenue
Woburn, MA 01888
Household paints, painting
materials, and equipment.

Daniel Smith
4150 First Avenue South
P.O. Box 84268
Seattle, WA 98124-5568
Do-it-yourself supplies. Mail
order. Catalog.

Fine Paints of Europe
P.O. Box 419
Woodstock, VT 05091
800-300-1556
Importers and distributors of
fine European paints. Call for
nearest retailer. Mail order.

Graphik Dimensions Ltd.
2103 Brentwood Street
High Point, NC 27263
800-221-0262
Do-it-yourself supplies and
materials. Mail order available.
Call for catalog.

Home Depot
449 Roberts Court Road
Kennisaw, GA 30144
Paints, equipment, and
materials for home decorating.

Janovic
30-35 Thompson Avenue
Long Island City, NY 11101
Large color choice of paints.

New York Central Art Supply
62 Third Avenue
New York, NY 10003
212-473-7705
Artist's materials and supplies.
Mail order. Call for catalog.

Pearl Paint Company, Inc.
306 Canal Street
New York, NY 10013-2572
800-221-6845
Many different colors of
household paints. Mail order.
Call for catalog.

Pittsburgh Paints
PPG Industries, Inc.
1PPG Place
Pittsburgh, PA 15272
Good choice of colors.

Pratt & Lambert
75 Townawanda Street
Buffalo
New York, NY 142007
Good color choice, plus a
good selection of off-whites.

Ralph Lauren Paint
980 Madison Avenue
New York, NY 10021
Huge collection of wonderful
colors and finishes. Catalog.

Sanderson
979 Third Avenue
New York, NY 10022
Large color choice of
own-brand paints.

Sherwin Williams
101 Prospect Avenue
Cleveland, OH
Good variety of colors for
household paints.

furniture and wooden accessories

Crate & Barrel
P.O. Box 9059
Wheeling, IL 60090-9059
800-451-8217
Good value furniture and
accessories.

IKEA
Ikea Catalog Department
185 Discovery Drive
Colmar, PA 18915
Offers a wide range of stylish
yet reasonably priced bare
wood furniture and accessories
of Swedish origin.

La Barge
Dept H90
P.O. Box 6917
Holland, MI 49422
Furniture and accessories with
old pine finishes.

Palecek
P.O. Box 225
Richmond, CA 94808
800-274-7730
Manufacturers of fine crafted
wicker and wooden accent
furniture. Call for a dealer in
your area.

The publishers and the author
of *Painted Furniture* are not
responsible for the products
sold by the companies listed
above, and it is not our
intention to promote any of
these purveyors.

glossary

Acetate transparent plastic film for stencils.

Artist's brushes good-quality brushes from art supply stores.

Artist's oil paint oil-based strong colors in tube form, used for tinting oil-based scumble.

Cissing paint will not adhere to the surface; remains in tiny globules. May occur when using vinegar paint.

Combing a paint technique that uses a combing tool, drawn over wet colored glaze to create wavy lines, zigzags or swirls.

Concentrated artist's acrylic strong water-based paint that can be mixed with other colors, glazes, or water.

Conté soft crayonlike pastel or pencil, used for marking.

Crackle glaze oil-based or water-based transparent glaze applied between layers of paint to produce a cracked effect.

Decorator's tape good variety of widths available. It is a low-tack tape, ideal for masking and protecting painted areas.

Dusting brush (*see* Stippling brush).

Eggshell paint water-based and oil-based, available in a nearly flat finish in a large color range. Used to paint woodwork.

Latex paint water-based mixed with a PVA resin and available in either flat or silk vinyl finishes. Available in a good color choice and often sold in small quantities that are perfect for painting and decorating small objects.

Masking tape low-tack is the best type of tape to use and it will not peel away the painted surface when removed. As an alternative, use decorator's tape. Both are available from art supply stores. Essential for masking panels and borders to be painted a different color. Used also for attaching stencils.

Pickling paste available as an oil-based or water-based wax, rubbed into wood, then wiped off for a light bleached look. Works especially well on wood with an open grain.

Plaka paint opaque traditional casein paint. It is water-based with a flat finish. Ideal for decorative details and can be thinned with water.

Powder paint finely ground pigments in a limited choice of vivid colors. Must be dissolved to use. Mix with water, sugar, and vinegar for vinegar painting.

Primer oil-based or water-based acrylic primer applied on top of bare wood to protect it so the surface is ready to paint.

Ragging creates a crumpled textured effect in a glaze using a crumpled cloth or plastic bag.

Registration marks drawn on stencils and tracings to serve as positioning guides.

Rubber-ended brush with wedged tip, used for creating patterns in wet, colored glazes.

Sandpaper available in various grits – fine, medium, and coarse. Used to smooth down woodwork ready for painting.

Satinwood paint a quick-drying water-based or oil-based paint with a low sheen finish. Large choice of colors available. Ideal for use on small items.

Scumble glaze oil-based and water-based glaze mixed with paint and used for broken colorwork such as graining and combing.

Sponge roller refill can be cut into a simple shape and used as a stamping tool.

Stencil card oiled manila card used for making stencils.

Stippling technique of repeated dabbing over wet, colored glazes to achieve a grainy effect that eliminates brush strokes.

Stippling brush wide bristled brush with stationary bridge handle used for stippling. A dusting brush is a similar and less expensive alternative.

Tracing paper semitransparent sheets of paper, used to copy and transfer outlines of motifs, patterns, and templates.

Varnishes oil-based and water-based, used to seal and protect painted woodwork.

Vinegar paint a homemade mixture of water, vinegar, sugar, and powder paint.

Whiting ground chalk that can be used to prevent cissing.

acknowledgments

First and foremost my heartfelt thanks to Tabby Riley—a gifted,
sensitive and intelligent painter; she gave so much to this book.
Also many thanks to David Montgomery for producing consistently
beautiful images with unstinting energy. To Tim Chapman, who crafted
most of the furniture with perception and undaunted enthusiasm.
Finally, to all at Ryland Peters and Small who put so much time and
effort into this book, and thanks especially to Victoria Holmes and
Maddalena Bastianelli.

Many thanks to the following persons and companies for lending us
furniture and accessories, so that we could paint and photograph
them: The Blue Door, The Dining Room Shop, Pavilion, Sasha Waddell,
Scumble Goosie, Shaker, and Tobias and the Angel.

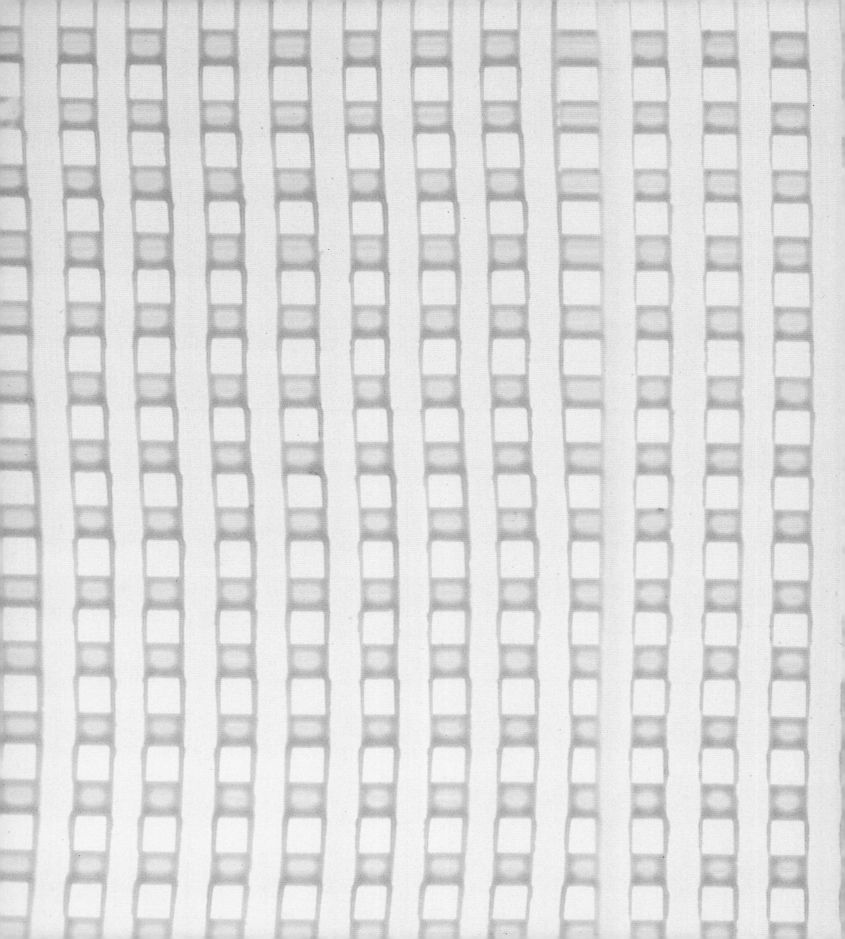